SIMPLY CHEROKEE:

Let's Learn
CHEROKEE
SYLLABARY

SIMPLY CHEROKEE:
Let's Learn CHEROKEE SYLLABARY

Marc W. Case

authorHOUSE®

AuthorHouse™
1663 Liberty Drive
Bloomington, IN 47403
www.authorhouse.com
Phone: 1-800-839-8640

© *2012 by Marc W. Case. All rights reserved.*

No part of this book may be reproduced, stored in a retrieval system, or transmitted by any means without the written permission of the author.

Published by AuthorHouse   07/10/2012

ISBN: 978-1-4772-4158-5 (sc)
ISBN: 978-1-4772-4157-8 (hc)
ISBN: 978-1-4772-4156-1 (e)

Library of Congress Control Number: 2012912510

Any people depicted in stock imagery provided by Thinkstock are models, and such images are being used for illustrative purposes only.
Certain stock imagery © Thinkstock.

Because of the dynamic nature of the Internet, any web addresses or links contained in this book may have changed since publication and may no longer be valid. The views expressed in this work are solely those of the author and do not necessarily reflect the views of the publisher, and the publisher hereby disclaims any responsibility for them.

Contents

Introduction 3

Trace the Syllabary 5

Review One 16

Review Two 30

Review Three 44

Review Four 58

Review Five 72

Review Six 86

Review Seven 100

Review Eight 114

Review Nine 122

About The Author 125

SimplyCherokee.com

Visit:

www.simplycherokee.com

for more information

SimplyCherokee.com

Introduction

Learning syllabary is the foundation of speaking, reading, and writing the Cherokee language fluently. The Cherokee syllabary is comprised of eighty-four characters, each character representing a vowel or a syllable.

This study associates each syllabary character with a simple story that contains a key word that triggers a unique sound, the syllabary's sound. Upon completing these lessons, when you see a syllabary character you will instantly recall its story and then impulsively say the appropriate sound. In the next book, "Simply Numbers" you will learn to put several sounds together, resulting in reading written Cherokee words. After that, Simply Cherokee lessons will cover complete sentences and everyday phrases.

Son of a Cherokee mother and an Apache father, I was raised by my mother's clan and spoke fluent Cherokee growing up. But it was not my family or my heritage that was the spark for this book. It was Japanese.

As a post-graduate, I relocated to Houston, where I served other veterans as a Veteran Service Representative at the Department of Veteran Affairs for seven years. While there a work opportunity presented itself to go to Japan; I jumped on it.

Prior to the trip I wanted to explore reading and writing Japanese and discovered the book: *Learn to Read and Write Japanese in a Weekend* by *Author Unknown*. Skeptical, I bought it and began reading the book on a Friday evening. By Monday morning I was reading Japanese and could write katagana and hiragana with confidence. Of course it wasn't magic; it was word association. I learned how to associate each Japanese character to something I already knew.

As a Cherokee speaker, I noticed many similarities between Cherokee and Japanese. Upon my return from Japan, I searched for a similar book that could teach Cherokee syllabary in a weekend. There was none. Like many Cherokees, I could speak the language but could not read nor write. This deficit in the Cherokee will mean the extinction of our word. Writing and reading is just as important as speaking. New Cherokee language speakers need an easy and fast way of learning syllabary if the language is to survive the next decade. This *Study of the Cherokee Syllabary* is just that: easy, fast, and effective.

Cherokee Sounds

Cherokee has 6 vowel sounds:

> "a" as in awful;
> "e" as in egg;
> "i" as in indian;
> "o" as in oval;
> "u" as in food
> "v" as in under

Several syllabary sounds do not exist or are challenging for English speakers to say. Don't worry, I'll keep it simple and let you know when they come up. There will be a note identifying when a sound is slightly altered.

Let's begin by tracing each of the 84 Cherokee syllabary characters.

Trace the Syllabary

Trace over each of these eighty-four Cherokee syllabary characters below. The order of the syllabary is from *Learn to Read & Write Cherokee in a Weekend*. Tracing the Cherokee syllabary will help you recognize each character as you learn it. It will seem familiar later as you are learning each lesson.

ᎦPLDGᏌᎢᎾYC
SᏚᏬᎠᎤᎤᏏᎠᏏᏆ
ᎯᏗᏟᏣᏬᎸᎣᏓᏪB
ᎨᎫGᏮᏲVᏫKtᏫ
ᎡᎤᏎMᎪᏮᏓᏝRL
ᎬᎪᏆᏪᏋᎧᏍᏠᏛᎤ
ᏔᏪᎴᎴᏬᏉVJᎥPR
ᏏᎡᎢᏇᎤᎴᎯᏃ
ᎣᎯᎴᏴ

SimplyCherokee.com

su Sounds Like sue

Lesson 1: There is a young girl named *Sue*. She has curly hair. One day while *Sue* was brushing her curly hair, she looked down and noticed a strand of her hair on the sink. The strand of curly hair *Sue* noticed in the sink looks exactly like this Cherokee syllabary and this is "su."

Every time you see this picture, remember: "Sue"

Practice writing and saying this syllabary on the lines below.

_____   _____   _____   _____

SimplyCherokee.com

Ii Sounds Like lee

Lesson 2: Sue has a pet frog she calls _Lee_. _Lee_ likes to leap around when he is on the ground. This syllabary is _Lee_ leaping. The straight line on the bottom represents the ground; the curved line going upward is the path of _Lee_'s leap; and the dot is _Lee_ the frog himself. This syllabary is "li" as in the name of Sue's frog.

Every time you see this picture, remember: "Lee"

Practice writing and saying this syllabary on the lines below.

_____   _____   _____   _____

SimplyCherokee.com

da Sounds Like **daw**

Lesson 3: Sue has friends from Europe who love to *dance* backward. They currently live in Jay. They don't say *dance* the way we do in Cherokee Country; they say *dahnce* because they're from Europe. When you see this backward looking letter J, think of Sue's European friends *Dahncing* backward in Jay. This syllabary is "da" as in the European-sounding word *dahncing*.

Every time you see this picture, remember: "Dahncing"

Practice writing and saying this syllabary on the lines below.

_____   _____   _____   _____

SimplyCherokee.com

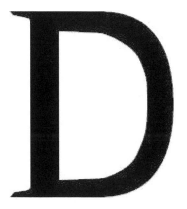

a Sounds Like ah

Lesson 4: Sue loves to practice archery. One day she was out shooting her bow and arrow and she shot her last arrow and lost it. Now Sue feels _awful_ because all she has is the bow and no arrows. Let this syllabary remind you of Sue's bow and her feeling _awful_ because she can't practice archery without arrows. This syllabary is "a" as in the word _awful_.

Every time you see this picture, remember: "Awful"

Practice writing and saying this syllabary on the lines below.

_____   _____   _____   _____

SimplyCherokee.com

lo Sounds Like low

Lesson 5: Sue's European friends invited her to a fancy party. The party is in the basement of a big house. Sue has to go _low_ down their spiral staircase to get to the party. This syllabary is "lo" as in the spiral staircase taking Sue _low_ to get to the party.

Every time you see this picture, remember: "Stairs go low"

Practice writing and saying this syllabary on the lines below.

_____   _____   _____   _____

SimplyCherokee.com

sa Sounds Like **saw**

Lesson 6: At the party Sue noticed that none of the food had any salt! Luckily she brought her own *saltshaker*, but the cork on the bottom had come loose and her *saltshaker* was empty. This looks like an empty, upside-down *saltshaker*. This syllabary is "sa" as in the word *saltshaker*.

Every time you see this picture, remember: "Saltshaker"

Practice writing and saying this syllabary on the lines below.

_____   _____   _____   _____

SimplyCherokee.com

i Sounds Like ee

Lesson 7: Sue's great grandmother was born in Tahlequah when it was _Indian_ Territory. It looks like the letter *T*, right? Think T for Territory and remember we live in what was once _Indian_ Territory. This syllabary is "i" as in the term _Indian_ Territory.

Every time you see this picture, remember: "Indian"

Practice writing and saying this syllabary on the lines below.

_____   _____   _____   _____

SimplyCherokee.com

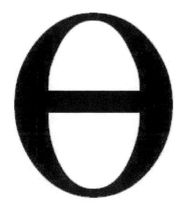 **na** Sounds Like **nah**

Lesson 8: Sue's favorite Mexican restaurant serves nachos in very big _nacho_ bowls. The bowls are divided into two sections: one is to hold the _nacho_ cheese, and the other is for chips. When you see this syllabary, think of Sue's _nacho_ dish with the cheese on one side and the chips on the other. This syllabary is "na" as in the word _nacho_.

Every time you see this picture, remember: "Nacho"

Practice writing and saying this syllabary on the lines below.

_____   _____   _____   _____

SimplyCherokee.com

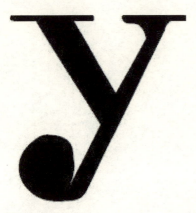

gi Sounds Like gih

Lesson 9: On Sue's first birthday, she received many gifts. The gift is represented by the dot and the lines are the arms of the elders handing baby sue her birthday gift as she sits on the floor surrounded by her gifts.

Every time you see this picture, remember: "Gift"

Practice writing and saying this syllabary on the lines below.

_____ _____ _____ _____

SimplyCherokee.com

tli Sounds Like cli

Lesson 10: *For story purposes, this sound is slightly altered.

Sue invented a new way to _clip_ her beautiful fingernails. This handy new invention is shaped like the letter *C*. Sue puts her nail inside the opening and squeezes the *C* together to _clip_ her nail. This syllabary looks like Sue's fingernail _clipping_ invention. This syllabary is "tli" and sounds like _cli_ as in the word _clip_.

Every time you see this picture, remember: "Clipper"

Practice writing and saying this syllabary on the lines below.

_____   _____   _____   _____

SimplyCherokee.com

Review One

Read each syllabary. Look at each syllabary and recall the story for each that you just learned. Review if needed. Practice remembering each story in your mind and say the corresponding sound.

ᏘᎮᏞᎠᏓᎨᎭᎳᎰᎽᏣ
ᎮᎴᎲᎳᎳᏔᏓᏴᎵᏓᏣᏘ
ᏓᎦᏘᎳᎮᎮᎭᎴᎠᏔᏴ

Read the Cherokee words below. To learn their meaning, click on the *Word List* at **www.simplycherokee.com**. Enter the Cherokee phonetics in the Cherokee field as you have learned and don't use spaces.

ᏘᎮ ᎠᎵ ᎠᎮ ᎽᏣ
ᏘᎵᎮ ᎰᎵ ᎠᏘᎦ ᎦᎦ
ᎭᎦᎮ ᎭᎭ ᎠᎮ ᎭᎮ

16

SimplyCherokee.com

Sound & Syllabary

Read each phrase below and pick out and underline the key word. The key words were underlined in each of the preceding stories. Write the syllabary sound in English, then write the Cherokee syllabary in the area provided.

Story	Sound	Cherokee Syllabary
1. Sue's curly hair	_____	_____
2. Sue's pet frog Lee likes to leap.	_____	_____
3. Dahancing backward in Jay	_____	_____
4. Sue feels awful.	_____	_____
5. The spiral staircase goes low.	_____	_____
6. Sue's empty saltshaker	_____	_____
7. Indian Territory	_____	_____
8. Sue's nacho dish	_____	_____
9. Sue's birthday gift	_____	_____
10. Sue's clipper invention	_____	_____

SimplyCherokee.com

Write the Syllabary

In Cherokee, write the correct syllabary in the space provided for each sound.

da   _____

su   _____

li   _____

sa   _____

lo   _____

a   _____

tli   _____

na   _____

i   _____

gi   _____

SimplyCherokee.com

Practice writing each syllabary. Write each corresponding Cherokee syllabary four times in the space provided.

su				
li				
da				
a				
lo				
sa				
i				
na				
gi				
tli				

SimplyCherokee.com

du Sounds Like dew

Lesson 11: Early in the morning the _dew_ falls. When it's windy the _dew_ swirls around. This is the path of the swirling _dew_ drop. The _dew_ swirls like the letter S. This syllabary is "du" just like the word _dew_.

Every time you see this picture, remember: "Dew"

Practice writing and saying this syllabary on the lines below.

_____   _____   _____   _____

SimplyCherokee.com

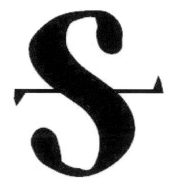

ga Sounds Like gaw

Lesson 12: Sue has a row of seed planted in her _garden._ Each morning the swirling dew falls on the _garden_. You can see the swirling dew from the last lesson, and the line across it represents Sue's row of seed planted in her _garden_. This syllabary is "ga" as in the word _garden_.

Every time you see this picture, remember: "Garden"

Practice writing and saying this syllabary on the lines below.

_____   _____   _____   _____

SimplyCherokee.com

S Sounds Like SS

Lesson 13: A sneaky snake saw Sue drop a potato in the garden. He wanted to taste it; so he decided to lick the potato. The circle part of this syllabary is the potato and the curved line is the sneaky snake licking the potato. After licking the potato, the snake said "<u>SS</u>," as sneaky snakes do. This syllabary is "<u>SS</u>."

Every time you see this picture, remember: "Sneaky snake"

Practice writing and saying this syllabary on the lines below.

_____   _____   _____   _____

SimplyCherokee.com

di Sounds Like **dee**

Lesson 14: Sue's little brother had stinky feet. Sue asks him, "_Did_ you wash your feet today?" He sticks a foot out to show her he _did_ indeed wash his stinky feet. Your imagination is required for this one. Imagine the _I_-shaped part of this syllabary is Sue's brother and the dot is his foot showing Sue that it has been washed. This syllabary is "di" as in the word _did_.

Every time you see this picture, remember: "Did"

Practice writing and saying this syllabary on the lines below.

_____   _____   _____   _____

SimplyCherokee.com

 u Sounds Like ooh

Lesson 15: Sue loves to go to a hog fry, and she likes to walk around and visit others while carrying her plate of _food_. It's difficult for her to carry her plate of _food_, fork, and drink while walking around, so she invented a new _food_ plate with a cup holder for her drink. The large ring is the _food_ plate, and the smaller ring is the cup holder. This syllabary is "oo" as in the word _food_.

Every time you see this picture, remember: "Food"

Practice writing and saying this syllabary on the lines below.

_____   _____   _____   _____

SimplyCherokee.com

nv Sounds Like **nuh**

Lesson 16: She also invented a bowl with a *nutcracker* attached because she got tired of hunting for it when there were nuts to be cracked. The ring is the bowl, and the clamp is the *nutcracker* device. This syllabary is "nv" as in the word *nutcracker*.

Every time you see this picture, remember: "Nutcracker"

Practice writing and saying this syllabary on the lines below.

_____   _____   _____   _____

si Sounds Like see

Lesson 17: Sue read in the newspaper about breaking news regarding small bees. This breaking news was that small bees can *see*. This syllabary resembles a small letter *b* that can *see*. This syllabary is "si" as in the word *see*.

Every time you see this picture, remember: "See"

Practice writing and saying this syllabary on the lines below.

_____ _____ _____ _____

O Sounds Like **oh**

Lesson 18: Here you see two <u>ovals</u>. The larger one is not quite complete and wearing a hat! <u>Ovals</u> can wear hats too.

Every time you see this picture, remember: "Oval"

Practice writing and saying this syllabary on the lines below.

_____ _____ _____ _____

SimplyCherokee.com

yo Sounds Like **yoh**

Lesson 19: Sue has a box full of *yo-yo*s. She filled it so full that one of the *yo-yo*s popped out. This syllabary resembles a *yo-yo* popping out of the box. The dot is the *yo-yo,* and the line is the string trailing behind. The curved line represents the box. This syllabary is "yo" as in the word *yo-yo*.

Every time you see this picture, remember: "Yo-yo"

Practice writing and saying this syllabary on the lines below.

_____ _____ _____ _____ _____

SimplyCherokee.com

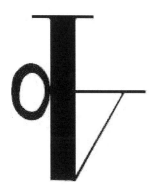

ha Sounds Like haw

Lesson 20: Sue has a top, but instead of spinning, this top _hops_ because it is lopsided. You can also think of it as an up-side-down number 4 _hopping_ on its head. Focus on the sound of the word _hopping_ and not the spelling. This syllabary is "ha" as in the word _hop_.

Every time you see this picture, remember: "Hop"

Practice writing and saying this syllabary on the lines below.

SimplyCherokee.com

Review Two

Read each syllabary. Look at each syllabary and recall the story for each that you just learned. Review if needed. Practice remembering each story in your mind and say the corresponding sound.

SЅⱷᎯᏞᎾᏫᏬᏏᏯᏂᏇ
ЅᏞᎾⱷᏏᏉᎾᏂᎯᏇЅ
ᏇЅᏥⱷᎾⱷᎯᎾᏉᏂᏞ

Below are Cherokee words. Click on the **Word List** at **www.simplycherokee.com** to learn their meanings. Enter the Cherokee phonetics in the Cherokee field as you have learned and don't use spaces.

ᎤᎿ ᏌᏚ ᎤᎾᏞ ᎤᎯ
ᏕᏕ ᎿᏕ ᏕᎯᎿᏝ ᏕᏌ
ᎯᏚᏞ ᏉᎾᏞ ᏥᏉ

SimplyCherokee.com

Sound & Syllabary

Read each phrase below and pick out and underline the key word. The key words were underlined in each of the preceding stories. Write the syllabary sound in English, then write the Cherokee syllabary in the area provided.

Story	Sound	Cherokee Syllabary
11. Dew swirling in the wind	_____	_____
12. Sue's row of seed in her garden	_____	_____
13. A sneaky snake saying "*SS*"	_____	_____
14. "Did you wash your feet?"	_____	_____
15. Sue's food plate invention	_____	_____
16. Sue's nutcracker invention	_____	_____
17. Small bees can see.	_____	_____
18. Small and large ovals.	_____	_____
19. A yo-yo popping out of the box	_____	_____
20. Sue's hopping top	_____	_____

SimplyCherokee.com

Write the Syllabary

In Cherokee, write the correct syllabary in the space provided for each sound.

du   _____

ga   _____

ss   _____

di   _____

oo   _____

nv   _____

o   _____

yo   _____

ha   _____

si   _____

SimplyCherokee.com

Practice writing each syllabary. Write each corresponding Cherokee syllabary four times in the space provided.

du				
ga				
ss				
di				
oo				
nv				
si				
o				
yo				
ha				

SimplyCherokee.com

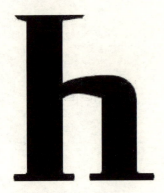

ni Sounds Like nee

Lesson 21: Sue's tall, skinny brother (Remember, he is the *I*) was playing with some friends and fell and hurt his <u>knee</u>. When you see this syllabary, let it remind you of the tall, skinny boy with his hurt <u>knee</u> extended. This syllabary sound is "ni" just like the word <u>knee</u>.

Every time you see this picture, remember: "Knee"

Practice writing and saying this syllabary on the lines below.

_____ _____ _____ _____

SimplyCherokee.com

ne Sounds Like neh

Lesson 22: All the kids went with Sue to the playground where there is a big slide. This is a picture of the slide. It was so fun that all the kids crowded to get on at once. An adult had to make them all line up, and when one finished sliding, the adult yelled, "_next_!". This syllabary is "ne" as in the word _next_!

Every time you see this picture, remember: "Next!"

Practice writing and saying this syllabary on the lines below.

_____   _____   _____   _____

wa Sounds Like **wah**

Lesson 23: Sue's mother is a great surgeon. When she washes her hands before surgery, she cannot touch anything, not even the *water* faucet handles. This is a special sink with foot pedals to turn off the *water*. The top part is the faucet where the *water* comes out; the flat part is the sink; and the bottom right is the foot pedal to turn the *water* off and on. This is "wa" as in the surgeon's *water* faucet with foot pedals.

Every time you see this picture, remember: "Water faucet"

Practice writing and saying this syllabary on the lines below.

_____   _____   _____   _____

SimplyCherokee.com

tsa Sounds Like **jaw**

Lesson 24: *For story purposes, this sound is slightly altered.

Imagine you have X-ray vision, and you see Sue's brother eating a *jaw* breaker. He has no teeth on the top of his mouth, represented by the flat line, and the round part is the *jaw* breaker itself. It has broken all his top teeth! This syllabary is "tsa," as in the word *jaw* breaker.

Every time you see this picture, remember: "Jaw breaker"

Practice writing and saying this syllabary on the lines below.

_____   _____   _____   _____

SimplyCherokee.com

ya Sounds Like **yah**

Lesson 25: Sue and her family went to the beach, where there were lots of waves. She wanted to measure the distance between the waves, so she used her _yardstick_. The small wave is in front and the big one is coming up behind. The yardstick is the crooked line in the middle. This syllabary is "ya" as in the word _yardstick._

Every time you see this picture, remember: "Yardstick"

Practice writing and saying this syllabary on the lines below.

_____   _____   _____   _____

SimplyCherokee.com

tsi Sounds Like **jii**

Lesson 26: *For story purposes, this sound is slightly altered.

Sue and her brother have a little neighbor friend named *Jim*. Sue's brother is taller than *Jim* and pats him on the head every time he comes over. Picture Sue's brother patting *Jim* on the head. This syllabary is "tsi" as in the name *Jim*.

Every time you see this picture, remember: "Jim"

Practice writing and saying this syllabary on the lines below.

_____ _____ _____ _____

SimplyCherokee.com

wi Sounds Like wee

Lesson 27: Sue's favorite movie is *The Wizard of Oz*. If you look closely at this syllabary, you can see the two letters *O* and *Z*, which spell Oz. (Hint: the *Z* is inside of the *O*.) When you see this syllabary, think of Sue's favorite movie. This syllabary is "wi" as in the word *wizard*.

Every time you see this picture, remember: "Wizard."

Practice writing and saying this syllabary on the lines below.

_____   _____   _____   _____

SimplyCherokee.com

qua Sounds Like **kwah**

Lesson 28: Sue has grown up and moved to the college dorm. There are four dorm rooms in each section, so they call them _quads_. This syllabary looks like two of the rooms: Sue's and her neighbor's. This syllabary is "qua" as in the word _quad_.

Every time you see this picture, remember: "Quad"

Practice writing and saying this syllabary on the lines below.

_____   _____   _____   _____

SimplyCherokee.com

we Sounds Like weh

Lesson 29: After college, Sue bought a house and decided to drill for _well_ water. This syllabary is a picture of her drill used to drill the hole. This syllabary is "we" as in the word _well_.

Every time you see this picture, remember: "Well"

Practice writing and saying this syllabary on the lines below.

_____   _____   _____   _____

SimplyCherokee.com

 yv Sounds Like yuh

Lesson 30: In her yard Sue has a yucca plant. She watched some big bees flying around the yucca. She determined the big bees love yucca plants and their blooms. This syllabary is "yv" as in the word *yucca*

Every time you see this picture, remember: "Young"

Practice writing and saying this syllabary on the lines below.

_____   _____   _____   _____

Review Three

Read each syllabary. Look at each syllabary and recall the story for each that you just learned. Review if needed. Practice remembering each story in your mind and say the corresponding sound.

ᏂᏌᏟᏞᏫᏋᎣᏓᏫᏐ
ᎣᏟᏓᏫᏋᏞᏞᏫᏐᏂ
ᏐᏓᏌᏋᏂᏋᎣᏞᏫᏫ

Below are Cherokee words. Click on the **Word List** at **www.simplycherokee.com** to learn their meanings. Enter the Cherokee phonetics in the Cherokee field as you have learned and don't use spaces.

ᏞᏋᏲ ᎠᏋᏓ ᎧᏫ ᏓᎣ
ᏤᎣᏫ ᏋᎴᏓ ᏲᏓ
ᏫᎻ ᎠᏐᎣᏫ

SimplyCherokee.com

Sound & Syllabary

Read each phrase below and pick out and underline the key word. The key words were underlined in each of the preceding stories. Write the syllabary sound in English, then write the Cherokee syllabary in the area provided.

Story	Sound	Cherokee Syllabary
21. Sue's brother hurt his knee	_____	_____
22. The adult yells, "NEXT!" at the slide	_____	_____
23. Surgeon's water facet has foot pedals	_____	_____
24. A jaw breaker knocked out his teeth	_____	_____
25. Sue measures waves with a yardstick	_____	_____
26. Sue's friend Jim.	_____	_____
27. *Wizard of Oz*	_____	_____
28. Sue's dorm room is in a quad	_____	_____
29. Sue's drill for well water	_____	_____
30. Big bees love yucca plants	_____	_____

SimplyCherokee.com

Write the Syllabary

In Cherokee, write the correct syllabary in the space provided for each sound.

wa   _____

ni   _____

ne   _____

tsa   _____

tsi   _____

ya   _____

we   _____

wi   _____

yv   _____

qua   _____

SimplyCherokee.com

Practice writing each syllabary. Write each corresponding Cherokee syllabary four times in the space provided.

ni				
ne				
wa				
tsa				
ya				
tsi				
wi				
qua				
we				
yv				

ge Sounds Like geh

Lesson 31: Sue's brother is back. Remember he is represented by the tall and skinny part of the syllabary that looks like the *I*. In this picture he is holding out his hand, and he wants you to *guess* what is in his hand. This syllabary is "ge" as in the word *guess*. When you see this picture, think of Sue's brother holding out his hand wanting you to *guess* what he is holding.

Every time you see this picture, remember: "Guess"

Practice writing and saying this syllabary on the lines below.

_____   _____   _____   _____

ti Sounds Like **tee**

Lesson 32: Sue's favorite restaurant has a fancy tea dispenser. The top part is where the _tea_ flows out and the bottom is where the drips of _tea_ are caught. This syllabary is "ti" just like the word _tea_. When you see this, think about the _tea_ dispenser at Sue's favorite restaurant.

WARNING: Don't confuse this with "di."

Every time you see this picture, remember: "Tea"

Practice writing and saying this syllabary on the lines below.

_____   _____   _____   _____

SimplyCherokee.com

yu Sounds Like you

Lesson 33: .Sue has an uncle named George, he has spiked hair. His hair is spiked because he is trying to reclaim his <u>youth</u>. This syllabary looks like a G as in George and you can see the spikes. Georges youth is important to him.

WARNING: Don't confuse this with "wa."

Every time you see this picture, remember: "Youth"

Practice writing and saying this syllabary on the lines below.

_____   _____   _____   _____

SimplyCherokee.com

tlo Sounds Like cloh

Lesson 34: *For story purposes, this sound is slightly altered.

Sue loves to cook with garlic _cloves_. She found this fancy garlic _clove_ press. The _cloves_ go in the bottom, and she presses down on the top part to squeeze the _cloves_. This syllabary is tlo and sounds like "clo," as in the word _clove_.

Every time you see this picture, remember: "Clove"

Practice writing and saying this syllabary on the lines below.

_____   _____   _____   _____

SimplyCherokee.com

ma Sounds Like mah

Lesson 35: When Sue was a baby, she loved to crawl under the table and take a nap. Her *ma* had to reach under and pick her up and put her to bed. This syllabary is "ma" like Sue' *ma*. The top part is the table, the loop represents baby Sue and the curvy line is *ma's* arm reaching to get Sue.

Every time you see this picture, remember: "Ma"

Practice writing and saying this syllabary on the lines below.

_____   _____   _____   _____

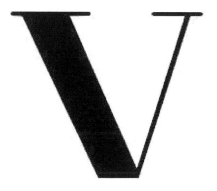

do Sounds Like **doe**

Lesson 36: At Cherokee Holiday Sue loves to eat funnel cake. The funnel cake vendors make _dough_ and squeeze it through a funnel. This is a picture of a funnel used to make the cake. All it needs is the _dough_. This syllabary is "do," as in the word _dough_.

Every time you see this picture, remember: "Dough"

Practice writing and saying this syllabary on the lines below.

_____ _____ _____ _____

SimplyCherokee.com

la _{Sounds Like} lah

Lesson 37: This syllabary looks like the letter *W*. When you see it, think of Washington D.C. In Washington, they make *laws*. This syllabary is "la," as in the word *laws* like they make in Washington.

Every time you see this picture, remember: "Laws"

Practice writing and saying this syllabary on the lines below.

_____ _____ _____ _____

SimplyCherokee.com

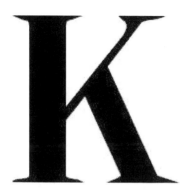

tso Sounds Like **joe**

Lesson 38: *For story purposes, this sound is slightly altered.

Sue's brother is back, again represented by the part of the syllabary shaped like the letter *I*. We find out his name is *Joe*. This is a picture of *Joe* flying a kite. The diagonal part going up is the kite string, and the diagonal part going down is *Joe*'s leg. It looks like the letter *K*, as in kite. This syllabary is "tso" and sounds like *Joe*.

Every time you see this picture, remember: "Joe"

Practice writing and saying this syllabary on the lines below.

_____   _____   _____   _____

SimplyCherokee.com

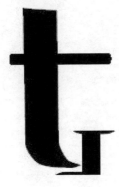

hna Sounds Like **hana**

Lesson 39: *For story purposes, this sound is slightly altered.*

Sue and Joe have a baby sister. Her name is Hanna, but Sue gave her a nickname. She calls her *Hna*. Just like Hanna but said quickly. This is a picture of *Hna* standing up in her baby chair with her arms outstretched. This syllabary is "hna" like Sue's nickname for baby Hanna.

Every time you see this picture, remember: "Hanna"

Practice writing and saying this syllabary on the lines below.

_____   _____   _____   _____

WO Sounds Like **woe**

Lesson 40: Sue and the kids go to the circus. There is an elephant eating peanuts but he got distracted. He used his trunk to pick up the peanut and almost dropped it in his eye. Sue yelled, "_Woah_ elephant! Don't put that peanut in your eye!" The dot is the peanut, the loop is the elephant's eye, and the curved line is the elephant's trunk. This syllabary is "wo" as in _woah_ elephant!

Every time you see this picture, remember: "_Woah_"

Practice writing and saying this syllabary on the lines below.

_____   _____   _____   _____

Review Four

Read each syllabary. Look at each syllabary and recall the story for each that you just learned. Review if needed. Practice remembering each story in your mind and say the corresponding sound.

ᎸᎫᎬᏨᏲ ᏤᏔᏮᏣᎤ
ᏧᏤᎬᎤᏲ ᏔᏯᎸᎫ
ᎤᏲᎸᏮᎫᎬᏨᏤᏔ

Below are Cherokee words. Click on the **Word List** at **www.simplycherokee.com** to learn their meanings. Enter the Cherokee phonetics in the Cherokee field as you have learned and don't use spaces.

ᏮᏔ ᎠᏲ ᏤᎰ ᏣᏪᎩ
ᏰᏞ ᎠᏞᏣᏱ ᎤᎫᏞ
ᏥᏩᏢ ᏯᎬ ᎠᎤᏢ

SimplyCherokee.com

Sound & Syllabary

Read each phrase below and pick out and underline the key word. The key words were underlined in each of the preceding stories. Write the syllabary sound in English, then write the Cherokee syllabary in the area provided.

Story	Sound	Cherokee Syllabary
31. Guess what is in his hand.	____	____
32. The tea dispenser	____	____
33. George's youthful spiked hair	____	____
34. Sue's fancy new garlic clove press	____	____
35. Sue's ma reaches under the table	____	____
36. Funnel cake dough	____	____
37. Laws are made in Washington D.C	____	____
38. Joe flies his kite.	____	____
39. Sue's baby sister "hna."	____	____
40. Woah, elephant!	____	____

SimplyCherokee.com

Write the Syllabary

In Cherokee, write the correct syllabary in the space provided for each sound.

yu   _____

ge   _____

ti   _____

do   _____

tlo   _____

ma   _____

wo   _____

la   _____

tso   _____

hna   _____

SimplyCherokee.com

Practice writing each syllabary. Write each corresponding Cherokee syllabary four times in the space provided.

ge				
ti				
yu				
tlo				
ma				
do				
la				
tso				
hna				
wo				

 nu Sounds Like new

Lesson 41: Sue was out shopping and noticed a _new_ product display in the store. The empty space between the flat lines is where the _new_ product goes. This is a picture of the display that Sue saw. When you see this picture of the _new_ items on display at the store, think of the Cherokee sound "nu." This syllabary is "nu" just like the word _new_.

Every time you see this picture, remember: "New"

Practice writing and saying this syllabary on the lines below.

_____ _____ _____ _____

 ka Sounds Like kaw

Lesson 42: One day Sue caught a cold and she <u>coughs</u> a lot. Imagine the larger ring as Sue's face and the smaller loop as her fist covering her mouth when she <u>coughs.</u>

This syllabary is "ka" as in the word <u>cough</u>. Focus on the sound of the word <u>cough</u>, not the English spelling.

Every time you see this picture, remember: "Cough"

Practice writing and saying this syllabary on the lines below.

_____   _____   _____   _____

SimplyCherokee.com

se Sounds Like seh

Lesson 43: This syllabary looks like the number four. When Sue bought a _set_ of dishes, she notices there were four of every type of dish. This syllabary is "se" as in the word _set_.

Every time you see this picture, remember: "Set"

Practice writing and saying this syllabary on the lines below.

_____ _____ _____ _____

SimplyCherokee.com

lu Sounds Like loo

Lesson 44: Sue learned to weave blankets using a *loom*. When she first began learning, she had the string all tangled up and going everywhere, this is a picture of Sue's *loom* with the string going everywhere. The outer vertical lines are the *loom* and the diagonal lines are the strings all tangled up. Or you can remember that the letter *M* ends the word *loom*, and that beginning is *loo*. This syllabary is "lu" as in the word *loom*.

Every time you see this picture, remember: "Loom"

Practice writing and saying this syllabary on the lines below.

_____   _____   _____   _____

dv Sounds Like **duh**

Lesson 45: On vacation, Sue enjoys going to Mardi Gras in New Orleans. She made a great mask to wear. The large loop on the left is the handle, and the top part is where she looks through the mask. When she is <u>*done*</u> with the mask, she stores it away for next year. This syllabary is "dv," as in the word *done*.

Every time you see this picture, remember: "Done"

Practice writing and saying this syllabary on the lines below.

_____ _____ _____ _____

SimplyCherokee.com

dla Sounds Like **dalaw**

Lesson 46: *For story purposes, this sound is slightly altered.

Stretch your imagination for this story! Sue passed by a doughnut shop where she saw two members of _da law_ (the law), police officers. They were sharing a doughnut. In this syllabary, the two loops at the bottom are the cops, the loop at the top is the doughnut, and they represent _da law_ (the law). This syllabary is "dla" and sounds like _da law_ (the law).

Every time you see this picture, remember: "Da law"

Practice writing and saying this syllabary on the lines below.

_____   _____   _____   _____

hi Sounds Like **hee**

Lesson 47: In the winter after a snow storm, Sue and Joe love to sled down the _hill_. This is a picture of Sue and Joe racing down a _hill_ on their sleds. The dots are Sue and Joe, and the lines are the trails in the snow where they slid. This syllabary is "hi," as in the word _hill_.

Every time you see this picture, remember: "Hill"

Practice writing and saying this syllabary on the lines below.

_____ _____ _____ _____

SimplyCherokee.com

 **ye** Sounds Like **yeh**

Lesson 48: This is a picture of a fancy *B*. Imagine this as a fancy bee, and it is a <u>*yellow*</u> jacket bee. Sue says they are the fanciest of bees. This syllabary is "ye" as in the word <u>*yellow*</u> jacket.

WARNING: Don't confuse this with "yv."

Every time you see this picture, remember: "Yellow"

Practice writing and saying this syllabary on the lines below.

_____ _____ _____ _____

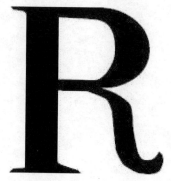

e Sounds Like eh

Lesson 49: Sue loves Chinese food. Her favorite is the *egg* roll. This syllabary looks like the letter *R*. When you see it, think rolls as in *egg* rolls, Sue's favorite Chinese food. This syllabary is "e," as in the term *egg* roll.

Every time you see this picture, remember: "Egg"

Practice writing and saying this syllabary on the lines below.

___ ___ ___ ___ ___ ___

SimplyCherokee.com

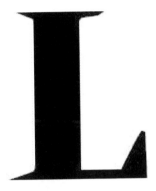

tle Sounds Like **cleh**

Lesson 50: *For story purposes, this sound is slightly altered.

This is a picture of a lever that was _cleverly_ designed. It is used by kings and queens to open a trapdoor people unwittingly stand on. The king or queen opens the trapdoor beneath subjects that complain too much. It is their _clever_ lever. This syllabary is "tle" and sounds like "cle," as in the word _clever_.

Every time you see this picture, remember: "Clever"

Practice writing and saying this syllabary on the lines below.

_____ _____ _____ _____ _____

Review Five

Read each syllabary. Look at each syllabary and recall the story for each that you just learned. Review if needed. Practice remembering each story in your mind and say the corresponding sound.

ᎤᎣᎨᎷᎶᏍᎦᎠᏏᎡᏞ

ᎷᏍᎠᎨᎴᎣᎺᏞᎸᎶᏰ

ᎠᎴᎣᎷᎦᏰᏞᎸᎨᎶ

Below are Cherokee words. Click on the **Word List** at **www.simplycherokee.com** to learn their meanings. Enter the Cherokee phonetics in the Cherokee field as you have learned and don't use spaces.

ᎠᏍᏫ ᎣᏂᏫᎶ ᎨᎷᏏᏍ

ᎤᏍᏇ ᏊᏪ ᎤᏣᎰ ᎴᎨ

ᎠᎵ ᏒᏣᎠ ᎠᏞᎠᎵ

SimplyCherokee.com

Sound & Syllabary

Read each phrase below and pick out and underline the key word. The key words were underlined in each of the preceding stories. Write the syllabary sound in English, then write the Cherokee syllabary in the area provided.

Story	Sound	Cherokee Syllabary
41. The new product display	_____	_____
42. Sue covers her cough.	_____	_____
43. Four dishes in a set	_____	_____
44. Sue's loom with string everywhere	_____	_____
45. Sue is done with her Mardi Gras mask	_____	_____
46. Da law officers share a doughnut	_____	_____
47. Sliding down the hill	_____	_____
48. Yellow Jackets are the fanciest of bees	_____	_____
49. Egg Roll	_____	_____
50. The king and queen's clever lever	_____	_____

SimplyCherokee.com

Write the Syllabary

In Cherokee, write the correct syllabary in the space provided for each sound.

se   _____

nu   _____

ka   _____

lu   _____

dla   _____

dv   _____

e   _____

hi   _____

yv   _____

tle   _____

Practice writing each syllabary. Write each corresponding Cherokee syllabary four times in the space provided.

nu				
ka				
se				
lu				
dv				
dla				
hi				
yv				
e				
tle				

gv Sounds Like guh

Lesson 51: On many <u>guns</u> there is a way to line things up when aiming at a target. When Sue practices shooting her <u>gun</u>, she uses these sights so she can hit the target. This is a picture of the sights on Sue's <u>gun</u> perfectly aligned. Pretend the <u>gun</u> is lying on its side. The top and bottom are the frame of the sight and the middle part is at the end of the <u>gun</u> barrel. This syllabary is "gv" as in the word <u>gun</u>.

Every time you see this picture, remember: "Gun"

Practice writing and saying this syllabary on the lines below.

_____   _____   _____   _____

SimplyCherokee.com

go Sounds Like **goh**

Lesson 52: Sue wants to be an Astronaut and _go_ to outer-space. This syllbary looks like the letter *A* as in Astronaut. It is shaped like an early day space capsule. It also resembles an arrow pointing up, which is where Astronauts _go_. This syllabary is "go" as in the term, "Astronauts _go_ up."

WARNING: Don't confuse this with "hi."

Every time you see this picture, remember: "Go"

Practice writing and saying this syllabary on the lines below.

_____   _____   _____   _____

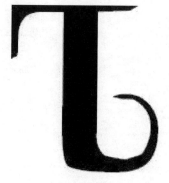 te Sounds Like teh

Lesson 53: Remember Sue's friends from Jay who dahanced backward? Well they dahanced backward all the way to *Texas*. This syllabary looks like the backward letter *J*, except with a little hook hanging on the left side. This syllabary is "te" as in the word *Texas*.

WARNING: Don't confuse this with "da."

Every time you see this picture, remember: "Texas"

Practice writing and saying this syllabary on the lines below.

_____ _____ _____ _____

ta Sounds Like tah

Lesson 54: At Cherokee Holiday there was a pair of _tall_ twins making funnel cakes. This syllabary looks like the two funnels they used to make the funnel cakes. This syllabary is "ta" as in the phrase "_tall_ twins."

WARNING: Don't confuse this with "la."

Every time you see this picture, remember: "Tall"

Practice writing and saying this syllabary on the lines below.

_____   _____   _____   _____

he Sounds Like heh

Lesson 55: When Joe was a little boy, represented by the smaller version of *I*, he always walked around with his hand on his _head_. This is a picture of little Joe with his hand on his head. This syllabary is "he" as in the word _head_.

Every time you see this picture, remember: "Head"

Practice writing and saying this syllabary on the lines below.

_____   _____   _____   _____

SimplyCherokee.com

 hu Sounds Like **who**

Lesson 56: Sue and Joe like to play a kids' game called hangman. This is the part of the game where they have drawn the gallows used to hang the looser. They ask, "<u>Who</u> is going to lose the game of hangman?" This syllabary is "hu" as in the word <u>who</u>.

Every time you see this picture, remember: "Who"

Practice writing and saying this syllabary on the lines below.

_____   _____   _____   _____

SimplyCherokee.com

de Sounds Like **deh**

Lesson 57: This one requires you to stretch your imagination. This syllabary looks like the letter *S*. Let's say the *S* is a gun slinging snake, and it has two guns making him _deadly_. A _deadly_ snake with his two guns! This syllabary is "de" as in the word _deadly_.

Every time you see this picture, remember: "Deadly"

Practice writing and saying this syllabary on the lines below.

____ ____ ____ ____

SimplyCherokee.com

SO Sounds Like **soe**

Lesson 58: Joe, represented by the *I* shape of this syllabary, is washing his hands with a bar of <u>soap</u> in each hand. This syllabary is "so" as in the word <u>soap</u>.

Every time you see this picture, remember: "Soap"

Practice writing and saying this syllabary on the lines below.

_____ _____ _____ _____

SimplyCherokee.com

tsu Sounds Like jew

Lesson 59: *For story purposes, this sound is slightly altered.

Sue went to a museum and saw ancient _Jewish_ clay pottery. This is a piece of a broken _Jewish_ wine bottle. Just the handle and spout remain. The container part for the wine has been broken off. This syllabary is "tsu" as in the term _Jewish_ wine bottle handle and spout.

Every time you see this picture, remember: "Jewish"

Practice writing and saying this syllabary on the lines below.

_____ _____ _____ _____

SimplyCherokee.com

qui Sounds Like **kwii**

Lesson 60: Joe was supposed to be working on his homework, but instead he was doodling, making funny faces on his paper. This is the funny face he was drawing of Sue and her pigtails but didn't finish because Sue caught him and made him *quit*. She said to him, "*Quit* drawing funny faces and get to work!" This syllabary is "qui," as in the word *quit*.

Every time you see this picture, remember: "Quit"

Practice writing and saying this syllabary on the lines below.

_____ _____ _____ _____

Review Six

Read each syllabary. Look at each syllabary and recall the story for each that you just learned. Review if needed. Practice remembering each story in your mind and say the corresponding sound.

ᎬᎠᏓᏪᏪᏆᏍᏛᎫᏊ

ᎫᏪᏗᏛᎠᏊᏢᎡᏓᏎ

ᏆᎪᏇᏎᏊᏆᏓᏢᎡᏫᏛ

Below are Cherokee words. Click on the **Word List** at **www.simplycherokee.com** to learn their meanings. Enter the Cherokee phonetics in the Cherokee field as you have learned and don't use spaces.

ᏪᏆ ᏊᎠᏪ ᏛᎠᏪ ᎠᏛ
ᏬᎠᏉ ᏪᏆᏬᎠᏉ ᎡᏢᏓ
ᎡᏆ ᏣᏆᏉ ᎠᏌᏪ

SimplyCherokee.com

Sound & Syllabary

Read each phrase below and pick out and underline the key word. The key words were underlined in each of the preceding stories. Write the syllabary sound in English, then write the Cherokee syllabary in the area provided.

Story	Sound	Cherokee Syllabary
51. Sue's gun is perfectly aligned	_____	_____
52. Astronauts go up to space.	_____	_____
53. Dahanced backward to Texas	_____	_____
54. The tall twins' funnels	_____	_____
55. Little Joe's hand on his head	_____	_____
56. Who is going to lose at Hangman?	_____	_____
57. A deadly snake	_____	_____
58. Bars of soap in each hand	_____	_____
59. Jewish wine bottle handle and spout	_____	_____
60. Quit drawing funny faces!	_____	_____

SimplyCherokee.com

Write the Syllabary

In Cherokee, write the correct syllabary in the space provided for each sound.

te   _____

gv   _____

go   _____

hu   _____

ta   _____

he   _____

qui   _____

de   _____

tsu   _____

so   _____

SimplyCherokee.com

Practice writing each syllabary. Write each corresponding Cherokee syllabary four times in the space provided.

gv				
go				
te				
ta				
he				
hu				
de				
so				
tsu				
qui				

SimplyCherokee.com

no Sounds Like **noe**

Lesson 61: Sue likes to read the comics. In the comics when someone is sleeping, several *Z*s are drawn above the person's head. Sue is teaching Joe the syllabary, and he is falling asleep. She yells, "*No* sleeping in Cherokee class!" This syllabary is "no," as in the word *no*, and it looks like the *ZZZ* in the comics when someone is sleeping.

Every time you see this picture, remember: "No!"

Practice writing and saying this syllabary on the lines below.

_____ _____ _____ _____

SimplyCherokee.com

 **que** Sounds Like **kweh**

Lesson 62: Sue went to *Quebec* in the summer and took a bike ride into and around the city. This is the map of the bike route she rode. She saw all the beautiful buildings in *Quebec* on her ride. This syllabary is "que," as in the city of "*Quebec*."

Every time you see this picture, remember: "Quebec"

Practice writing and saying this syllabary on the lines below.

_____   _____   _____   _____

SimplyCherokee.com

Ꭵ Sounds Like uh

Lesson 63: Sue, Joe, and Hna went to a Civil War reenactment. There, they saw a cannon and a cannonball. Sue took a picture of the cannon just as the ball was shooting out. This is a picture of the cannon _under_ the cannon ball. This syllabary is "v," and it sounds like "uh," as in the word _under_. Every time you see this picture, remember: "Under"

Practice writing and saying this syllabary on the lines below.

_____   _____   _____   _____

SimplyCherokee.com

ho Sounds Like hoe

Lesson 64: It is spring time now and Joe wants to plant a garden. Sue gave him a brand new garden *hoe* to help him. This is Joe, represented by the *I*, holding his new *hoe*. This syllabary is "ho," as in the word *hoe*.

Every time you see this picture, remember: "Hoe"

Practice writing and saying this syllabary on the lines below.

_____   _____   _____   _____

le Sounds Like **leh**

Lesson 65: Sue and the kids like to travel. They went to Hawaii for the first time. At the airport in Hawaii, everyone receives a free *lei*. Of course a *lei* is a necklace made of fresh flowers. In their hotel room there is a *lei* hanger; this is used to keep the *lei* fresh. The top part hooks over the door and the loop part is where one hangs the *lei* to keep it aired out and fresh. This syllabary is "le" as in the term *lei* hanger.

Every time you see this picture, remember: "Lei"

Practice writing and saying this syllabary on the lines below.

_____   _____   _____   _____

SimplyCherokee.com

tse Sounds Like **jeh**

Lesson 66: *For story purposes, this sound is slightly altered.

In Hawaii, Joe is playing with his toy *jet*. He pretends it crashed and bounced back into the air. This picture is Joe's toy *jet*, up-side-down, it crashes and bounces back into the air. This syllabary is "tse" as in the word *jet*.

Every time you see this picture, remember: "Jet"

Practice writing and saying this syllabary on the lines below.

_____   _____   _____   _____

SimplyCherokee.com

gu Sounds Like **goo**

Lesson 67: Back in Jay, the _gurus_ are hard at work trying to learn to dahnce backward, but they can't! The _gurus_ can only dahnce forward. In Jay, there are many _gurus_. This syllabary is "gu," as in the word _guru_, and this syllabary looks like the letter J.

Every time you see this picture, remember: "Guru"

Practice writing and saying this syllabary on the lines below.

_____ _____ _____ _____

quo Sounds Like kwoh

Lesson 68: Upon their return from Hawaii, the news reporters wanted to get a *quote* from Sue about her recent vacation. As an educated professional, Sue gave an elegant vocal *quote*. "Cherokee people must learn to exchange our culture, language, and history. That is my *quote*." This syllabary is "quo," as in the word *quote*. The V part represents vocal, and the flair makes it elegant.

Every time you see this picture, remember: "Quote"

Practice writing and saying this syllabary on the lines below.

_____   _____   _____   _____

tlv Sounds Like cluh

Lesson 69: Remember Joe, represented by the *l*? Well, now he is twenty-one, and he decided to go to a *club*. The bouncer didn't believe he was twenty-one, so he *clubbed* him with a *club* and told him to "get lost!" This is Joe with a swollen eye that he got at the *club*. This syllabary is "tlv" as in the word *club*.

Every time you see this picture, remember: "Club"

Practice writing and saying this syllabary on the lines below.

_____   _____   _____   _____

SimplyCherokee.com

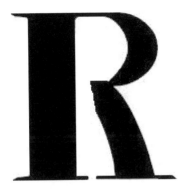 sv Sounds Like **suh**

Lesson 70: When Joe got clubbed, he dropped _something_. This is a picture of Joe using his foot looking for _something_ he dropped because he can't see. This syllabary is "sv" as in the word _something_.

WARNING: Don't get this confused with "e."

Every time you see this picture, remember: "Something"

Practice writing and saying this syllabary on the lines below.

_____   _____   _____   _____

SimplyCherokee.com

Review Seven

Read each syllabary. Look at each syllabary and recall the story for each that you just learned. Review if needed. Practice remembering each story in your mind and say the corresponding sound.

ZᏯiᏮᏙᏙᎫᏑᏤ ᏢᏒ

ᏤᎡᏓiᏢᏙᏬᎡᏃᏛ

ᎵᏤiᏗᏛᏢᏬᎡᏃᏙ

Below are Cherokee words. Click on the **Word List** at **www.simplycherokee.com** to learn their meanings. Enter the Cherokee phonetics in the Cherokee field as you have learned and don't use spaces.

ᏍᎵᏤᎩ iᎾᎷ ᎨᎦ
ᏲᏛ ᏲᏑᎳᏬᎷ ᎠᏍ
ᎠᏬᏍ ᏗᏑ

100

SimplyCherokee.com

Sound & Syllabary

Read each phrase below and pick out and underline the key word. The key words were underlined in each of the preceding stories. Write the syllabary sound in English, then write the Cherokee syllabary in the area provided.

Story	Sound	Cherokee Syllabary
61. No sleeping!	_____	_____
62. Sue's bike path in Quebec	_____	_____
63. The cannon is under the cannon ball	_____	_____
64. Joe with his garden hoe	_____	_____
65. Lei hanger	_____	_____
66. Joe's toy jet	_____	_____
67. The gurus from Jay	_____	_____
68. Sue's elegant vocal quote	_____	_____
69. Joe's swollen eye from the club	_____	_____
70. He used his foot looking for something	_____	_____

Write the Syllabary

In Cherokee, write the correct syllabary in the space provided for each sound.

v   _____

no   _____

que   _____

le   _____

tse   _____

ho   _____

sv   _____

tlv   _____

gu   _____

quo   _____

SimplyCherokee.com

Practice writing each syllabary. Write each corresponding Cherokee syllabary four times in the space provided.

no				
que				
v				
ho				
le				
tse				
gu				
quo				
tlv				
sv				

SimplyCherokee.com

yi Sounds Like yee

Lesson 71: Sue told Joe that he has to use his brain. She challenged him to invent something new. So, he invented a remote-controlled table that _yields_ before hitting anything. This is Joe's table, represented by the top part. The wheel is the circle in the bottom right corner, and the breaks, or _yielding_ mechanism, is the checkmark in the bottom left. This syllabary is "yi," as in the word _yield_.

Every time you see this picture, remember: "Yield"

Practice writing and saying this syllabary on the lines below.

_____   _____   _____

SimplyCherokee.com

lv Sounds Like luh

Lesson 72: As Sue ages, she notices her *love* handles. She feels fat. In her mind, this is a picture of her *love* handle. Sue hangs her head, sad, as she examines her handle, then decides to eat healthy, exercise, and get rid of the handles of *love*. This syllabary is "lv," as in the term *love* handle.

Every time you see this picture, remember: "Love"

Practice writing and saying this syllabary on the lines below.

_____   _____   _____   _____

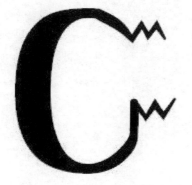

tsv Sounds Like **juh**

Lesson 73: *For story purposes, this sound is slightly altered.

Hna and Joe enjoy *jumping* on the trampoline in Sue's back yard. The *C* part is the trampoline, and the squiggly lines are Hna and Joe *jumping*. This syllabary is "tsv," as in the word *jump*.

Every time you see this picture, remember: "Jump"

Practice writing and saying this syllabary on the lines below.

_____ _____ _____ _____

SimplyCherokee.com

tlu Sounds Like **clue**

Lesson 74: *For story purposes, this sound is slightly altered.

Joe found his old drawing of a funny face. Sue kept it. Now, he is a professional detective, and he draws a scope to show he is looking for _clues_ to solve his cases. This is Joe's funny face using a scope, in the upper left hand corner, looking for _clues_. This syllabary is "tlu" as in the word _clue_.

WARNING: Don't confuse this with "hv."

Every time you see this picture, remember: "Clue"

Practice writing and saying this syllabary on the lines below.

_____   _____   _____   _____

quu Sounds Like kwoo

Lesson 75: *For story purposes, this sound is slightly altered and is not common in English.

Baby Hna loves to ride roller coasters. Hna only understands Cherokee so she doesn't coo like English babies, instead, she says "*quu*." This is a picture of Hna on a roller coaster having a great time, and she says "*quu*" like babies do when they are happy. The dot is Hna on the roller coaster, and the curved lines are the roller coaster rails. This syllabary is "*quu*," as in the Cherokee baby sound.

Every time you see this picture, remember: "Coo/Quu"

Practice writing and saying this syllabary on the lines below.

_____ _____ _____ _____

SimplyCherokee.com

tla Sounds Like **claw**

Lesson 76: *For story purposes, this sound is slightly altered.

Education is extremely important to Sue, Joe, and baby Hna. They learned about how sundials were used as ancient _clocks_. Let this picture represent an ancient _clock_. The dot represents the sun, the bottom is the dial itself, and the line connecting the sun to the dial at the bottom is the sun's rays. This syllabary is "tla," as in the word _clock_.

Every time you see this picture, remember: "Clock"

Practice writing and saying this syllabary on the lines below.

_____ _____ _____ _____

quv Sounds Like **kwuh**

Lesson 77: *For story purposes, this sound is slightly altered.

Hna loves the ocean. She wants to become an <u>aqua</u> marine biologist. When the family went to the beach, she found an eel about to make its transition. This is a picture of the eel all curled up and dried out. It is the inspiration for Hna to study <u>aqua</u> marine biology. She wants to save the eels. This syllabary is "quv," as in the last part of the English word <u>aqua</u>. Also, it looks like the letter *E*, as in the English word eel.

Every time you see this picture, remember: "Aqua"

Practice writing and saying this syllabary on the lines below.

_____   _____   _____   _____

hv Sounds Like huh

Lesson 78: Joe is an adult now and decides to *hunt* those deadly snakes. This is grown up Joe, represented by the cursive *l*, holding a rifle as if he is *hunting*. The flat part of this picture on the right represents the rifle. This syllabary is "hv," as in the word *hunt.*

WARNING: Don't get this confused with "tlu."

Every time you see this picture, remember: "Hunt"

Practice writing and saying this syllabary on the lines below.

_____   _____   _____   _____

WU Sounds Like **WOO**

Lesson 79: Sue pays great attention to detail. When she saw the movie *Star Wars*, she noticed there were nine different <u>Wookies</u>, the Chewbacca characters. This syllabary is "wu," as in the word <u>Wookie</u>, and looks like the number nine, as Sue noticed.

Every time you see this picture, remember: "Wookies"

Practice writing and saying this syllabary on the lines below.

_____   _____   _____   _____

SimplyCherokee.com

 **Wv** Sounds Like **wuh**

Lesson 80: Sue also watched the movie, *Alice in <u>Wonderland</u>*. To her surprise, there were not six witches in <u>Wonderland</u>. She expected to count at least six witches in <u>Wonderland</u>, but there where none. This syllabary is "wv," as in the word <u>Wonderland</u>, and it looks like the number six.

Every time you see this picture, remember: "Wonderland"

Practice writing and saying this syllabary on the lines below.

_____   _____   _____   _____

SimplyCherokee.com

Review Eight

Read each syllabary. Look at each syllabary and recall the story for each that you just learned. Review if needed. Practice remembering each story in your mind and say the corresponding sound.

ᏏᎡᏨᏇᏫᏞᏋᏉᏟ
ᎡᏇᏞᏋᏨᏉᎡᏈᏏᏫ
ᏋᏏᏋᎡᏞᏇᏫᎡᏉᏨ

Below are Cherokee words. Click on the **Word List** at www.simplycherokee.com to learn their meanings. Enter the Cherokee phonetics in the Cherokee field as you have learned and don't use spaces.

ᎿᏫ ᏉᏚᏢᎬ ᏍᏚᏃᏈ
ᏭᏏ ᎤᏁᏆᎳᏫᏆ

SimplyCherokee.com

Sound & Syllabary

Read each phrase below and pick out and underline the key word. The key words were underlined in each of the preceding stories. Write the syllabary sound in English, then write the Cherokee syllabary in the area provided.

Story	Sound	Cherokee Syllabary
71. Joe's table yields.	_____	_____
72. Sue's love handle	_____	_____
73. Hna & Joe jump on the trampoline	_____	_____
74. Use a scope to look for clues	_____	_____
75. Hna says "quu" on the rollercoaster	_____	_____
76. Ancient sundials were clocks	_____	_____
77. Aqua marine biologists save eels	_____	_____
78. Adult Joe hunts.	_____	_____
79. Nine wookies.	_____	_____
80. Expected six witches in Wonderland	_____	_____

SimplyCherokee.com

Write the Syllabary

In Cherokee, write the correct syllabary in the space provided for each sound.

tsv   _____

yi   _____

lv   _____

quu   _____

tla   _____

tlu   _____

quv   _____

wv   _____

hv   _____

wu   _____

SimplyCherokee.com

Practice writing each syllabary. Write each corresponding Cherokee syllabary four times in the space provided.

yi				
lv				
tsv				
tlu				
quu				
tla				
quv				
hv				
wu				
wv				

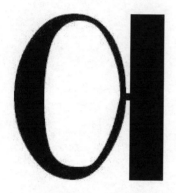

me Sounds Like meh

Lesson 81: This syllabary looks like the letter *O* and the letter *I*, as in the sentence, "Oh, I just _met_ him," which is what Sue said when her friend introduced her to another friend. This syllabary is "me," as in the word _met_.

Every time you see this picture, remember: "Met"

Practice writing and saying this syllabary on the lines below.

_____   _____   _____   _____

SimplyCherokee.com

mi Sounds Like **mee**

Lesson 82: This is Joe, represented by the *I* shapes in the image. Notice there are two. This is because Joe is looking at himself in a *mirror*. This syllabary is "mi," as in the word *mirror*.

Every time you see this picture, remember: "Mirror"

Practice writing and saying this syllabary on the lines below.

SimplyCherokee.com

mo Sounds Like **moe**

Lesson 83: Joe enjoys riding his unicycle, but today he can't because the wheel has a huge hole in it and makes the unicycle not _mobile_. This is a picture of Joe's unicycle with the seat at the top and the broken wheel at the bottom. This syllabary is "mo," as in the word _mobile_.

Every time you see this picture, remember: "Mobile"

Practice writing and saying this syllabary on the lines below.

_____   _____   _____   _____

SimplyCherokee.com

mu Sounds Like **moo**

Lesson 84: Sue bought a cow. There are two gates on her land that the cow has to pass to eat. The flat "dashes" in this picture are the gates on the top right and the bottom left. The diagonal line represents the cow passing the gates. As she passes, she says "_MOO_." This syllabary is "mu" as in "_MOO_" like the cow says.

Every time you see this picture, remember: "Moo"

Practice writing and saying this syllabary on the lines below.

____ ____ ____ ____

Review Nine

Read each syllabary. Look at each syllabary and recall the story for each that you just learned. Review if needed. Practice remembering each story in your mind and say the corresponding sound.

ᏧᎻᏊᏫ ᎻᏧᎬᎩ

ᏊᏧᎫ ᎻᎫ ᏧᎻᏊ

Below are Cherokee words. Click on the **Word List** at **www.simplycherokee.com** to learn their meanings. Enter the Cherokee phonetics in the Cherokee field as you have learned and don't use spaces.

ᏆᎻ   ᏧᏍ   ᏫᏔ   ᏊᏫ

SimplyCherokee.com

Sound & Syllabary

Read each phrase below and pick out and underline the key word. The key words were underlined in each of the preceding stories. Write the syllabary sound in English, then write the Cherokee syllabary in the area provided.

Story	Sound	Cherokee Syllabary
81. "Oh, I just met him," Sue said	_____	_____
82. Joe looks in a mirror.	_____	_____
83. Joe's unicycle is not mobile	_____	_____
84. The cows say "MOO" as they pass	_____	_____

Write the Syllabary

In Cherokee, write the correct syllabary in the space provided for each sound.

mo	_____
mu	_____
mi	_____
me	_____

SimplyCherokee.com

Practice writing each syllabary. Write each corresponding Cherokee syllabary four times in the space provided.

me			
mi			
mo			
mu			

Thank you for choosing Simply Cherokee to answer your Cherokee Language needs. You can download complete answer keys for each of the reviews at www.simplycherokee.com.

About The Author

Marc Case, half Cherokee and half Apache, was raised in a Cherokee-speaking home. After learning to read and write Japanese in a weekend, a language which also uses a syllabary, Marc developed similar tools for the Cherokee language in his Simply Cherokee line. Preserving our language preserves the foundation of the Cherokee civilization.

Made in the USA
Lexington, KY
18 October 2015